MAKING MONEY ONLINE: BOOK 7

BY MICHAEL CALLUM MAYAKA

ONLINE INVESTMENTS AND TRADING

FOREWORD:

In today's digital age, making money online has become a viable and accessible option for individuals seeking financial independence or additional income streams. The internet offers a plethora of opportunities that allow you to leverage your skills, creativity, and resources to generate revenue. This guide aims to provide you with valuable insights, strategies, and practical tips on how to make money online effectively.

This book is part of a series for more information see Further reading at the end of this book.

Table of Contents

Foreword: 3
7. Online Investments and Trading 5
   7.1 Stock Market and Day Trading: An Overview 6
      The Stock Market: 6
      Day Trading: 8
      Considerations for Stock Market and Day Trading: 11
      Conclusion: 13
   7.2 Cryptocurrency Trading and Investing: A Brief Overview 13
      Understanding Cryptocurrencies: 14
      Different Approaches to Cryptocurrency Investment: 15
      Key Considerations for Cryptocurrency Trading and Investing: 16
      Conclusion: 19
   7.3 Peer-to-Peer Lending and Crowdfunding 21
      Peer-to-Peer Lending: 22
      Crowdfunding: 24
      Tips for Success: 28
      Conclusion: 30
Further reading: 32

7. ONLINE INVESTMENTS AND TRADING

7.1 STOCK MARKET AND DAY TRADING: AN OVERVIEW

The stock market and day trading are two terms often associated with the world of finance and investing. Both concepts involve the buying and selling of financial instruments, primarily stocks, with the aim of generating profits. In this section, we will provide a brief overview of the stock market and day trading, including their key features, benefits, and considerations.

THE STOCK MARKET:

The stock market refers to the platform where investors buy and sell shares or ownership stakes in publicly traded companies. It acts as a marketplace where buyers and sellers come together to trade stocks. The stock market plays a crucial role in the economy by providing companies with access to capital and offering individuals an opportunity to invest in those companies.

Key Features of the Stock Market:

1. Publicly Traded Companies: The stock market primarily deals with shares of publicly traded companies. These companies go through an initial public offering (IPO) process to become listed on stock exchanges, allowing their shares to be traded by the public.

2. Stock Exchanges: Stock exchanges, such as the New York Stock Exchange (NYSE) and NASDAQ, provide a centralized platform for buying and selling stocks. These exchanges ensure transparency, liquidity, and fair pricing for investors.

3. Stock Indices: Stock indices, such as the S&P 500 and Dow Jones Industrial Average (DJIA), track the performance of a specific group of stocks. They serve as benchmarks to assess the overall market performance.

DAY TRADING:

Day trading is a short-term trading strategy that involves buying and selling financial instruments within the same trading day. Day traders aim to profit from small price fluctuations in stocks, currencies, commodities, or other assets. Unlike long-term investors, day traders are not concerned with the long-term value of a stock; instead, they focus on taking advantage of short-term market movements.

Key Features of Day Trading:

1. Short Holding Periods: Day traders typically hold positions for a few minutes to hours, closing all positions by the end of the trading day. They do not carry positions overnight to avoid overnight market risks.

2. Technical Analysis: Day traders heavily rely on technical analysis, using charts, indicators, and patterns to identify entry and exit points. They analyze historical price data and market trends to make short-term trading decisions.

3. High-Risk, High-Reward: Day trading can be highly volatile and involves significant risk. While it offers the potential for substantial profits in a short time, it also exposes traders to potential losses. Proper risk management and discipline are crucial for day traders.

CONSIDERATIONS FOR STOCK MARKET AND DAY TRADING:

1. Education and Research: It is essential to acquire a solid understanding of the stock market and day trading before engaging in these activities. Educate yourself about trading strategies, risk management, and market analysis techniques. Stay updated with financial news and market trends.

2. Risk Management: Both stock market investing and day trading involve risks. Develop a risk management plan to protect your capital and set realistic profit and loss targets. Use stop-loss orders to limit potential losses.

3. Emotional Discipline: Controlling emotions, such as fear and greed, is vital in stock market investing and day trading. Emotional decision-making can lead to impulsive trades and poor outcomes. Maintain discipline, stick to your trading plan, and avoid making decisions based on emotions.

4. Continuous Learning: The stock market is dynamic, and day trading strategies evolve. Stay open to learning, adapt to changing market conditions, and continuously improve your trading skills.

CONCLUSION:

The stock market and day trading offer opportunities for individuals to participate in financial markets and potentially generate profits. However, they require knowledge, discipline, and risk management. Whether you choose to invest in stocks for the long term or engage in day trading, it is crucial to approach these activities with a well-defined strategy, realistic expectations, and a commitment to continuous learning.

7.2 CRYPTOCURRENCY TRADING AND INVESTING: A BRIEF OVERVIEW

Cryptocurrency trading and investing have gained significant popularity in recent years, offering individuals the opportunity to participate in the fast-paced and dynamic world of digital currencies. This form of investment involves buying, selling, and holding cryptocurrencies with the aim of generating profits. In this section, we will explore the basics of cryptocurrency trading and investing, key considerations, and potential strategies.

UNDERSTANDING CRYPTOCURRENCIES:

Cryptocurrencies, such as Bitcoin, Ethereum, and Litecoin, are digital or virtual currencies that utilize cryptography for secure transactions, control the creation of new units, and verify the transfer of assets. They operate on decentralized networks known as blockchains, which provide transparency, security, and immutability.

DIFFERENT APPROACHES TO CRYPTOCURRENCY INVESTMENT:

1. Long-term Investment: This strategy involves purchasing cryptocurrencies with the intention of holding them for an extended period, typically months or even years. The aim is to benefit from potential long-term growth and value appreciation. Long-term investors believe in the potential of cryptocurrencies to revolutionize various industries and have faith in their continued adoption.

2. Short-term Trading: Short-term trading, also known as day trading, involves actively buying and selling cryptocurrencies within short timeframes, sometimes within a single day. Traders rely on technical analysis, market trends, and volatility to identify short-term price movements and generate profits from the price fluctuations.

KEY CONSIDERATIONS FOR CRYPTOCURRENCY TRADING AND INVESTING:

1. Research and Education: Before entering the cryptocurrency market, it is crucial to thoroughly research and understand the underlying technology, market dynamics, and potential risks. Stay updated with news,

follow industry experts, and learn about different cryptocurrencies to make informed decisions.

2. Risk Management: Cryptocurrency trading and investing carry inherent risks due to the highly volatile nature of the market. It is essential to establish a risk management strategy that includes diversification, setting stop-loss orders, and only investing what you can afford to lose.

3. Security: As cryptocurrencies are digital assets, security is of utmost importance. Implement robust security measures, such as using hardware wallets, enabling two-factor authentication, and practicing good

password hygiene. Be cautious of phishing attempts and ensure the platforms you use have proper security protocols.

4. Choosing a Reliable Exchange: Selecting a reputable cryptocurrency exchange is crucial for trading and investing. Consider factors such as security, liquidity, fees, user experience, and customer support. Conduct thorough research and read user reviews before choosing a platform.

5. Technical Analysis: For traders, understanding technical analysis can be beneficial. Analyze price charts, indicators, and patterns to identify potential entry and exit points. However, remember that

technical analysis is not foolproof, and market sentiment and external factors can influence prices.

6. Emotions and Discipline: Emotions can significantly impact trading decisions. It is essential to remain disciplined, avoid impulsive trades driven by fear or greed, and stick to your trading strategy. Emotional trading can lead to losses and poor decision-making.

CONCLUSION:

Cryptocurrency trading and investing offer exciting opportunities to participate in the ever-evolving digital currency market. Whether you choose long-term investment or short-term trading, it is crucial to conduct thorough research, practice risk management, and prioritize security. The cryptocurrency market is highly volatile and speculative, so exercise caution and only invest what you can afford to lose. By staying informed, adopting a disciplined approach, and continuously learning, you can navigate the world of cryptocurrency trading and investing with greater confidence.

7.3 PEER-TO-PEER LENDING AND CROWDFUNDING

Peer-to-peer lending and crowdfunding have emerged as powerful financial mechanisms that connect borrowers and investors in a mutually beneficial way. These online platforms have revolutionized the traditional lending and fundraising landscape by enabling individuals and businesses to access capital from a diverse pool of investors. In this section, we will explore the concepts of peer-to-peer lending and crowdfunding, their benefits, and how you can leverage these platforms to make money online.

PEER-TO-PEER LENDING:

Peer-to-peer (P2P) lending platforms facilitate direct lending between individuals or businesses without the involvement of traditional financial institutions. These platforms act as intermediaries, connecting borrowers seeking loans with investors looking to earn returns on their investments. P2P lending offers several advantages for both borrowers and lenders:

1. Access to Capital: P2P lending provides borrowers with an alternative source of funding when traditional banks may not be readily available or offer less favourable terms. It allows borrowers to access loans

quickly and conveniently, often at competitive interest rates.

2. Diversification and Returns: For lenders, P2P lending offers an opportunity to diversify their investment portfolio by allocating funds to multiple loans across various risk profiles. By spreading their investments, lenders can potentially earn higher returns compared to traditional savings accounts or bonds.

3. Transparency and Control: P2P lending platforms typically provide detailed information about borrowers' creditworthiness, loan terms, and repayment schedules. This transparency

empowers lenders to make informed decisions based on risk assessment and select loans that align with their investment goals.

4. Passive Income: Lenders can earn passive income through interest payments and fees generated by the loans they fund. Some platforms offer automated investment tools that allocate funds across a portfolio of loans, reducing the time and effort required for individual loan selection.

CROWDFUNDING:

Crowdfunding platforms allow individuals or businesses to raise funds from a large number of people, often through small contributions. Crowdfunding campaigns are commonly used for creative projects, entrepreneurial ventures, charitable causes, or personal needs. Here are the key benefits of crowdfunding:

1. Broad Investor Base: Crowdfunding enables entrepreneurs and creators to tap into a broad network of potential backers, including friends, family, and strangers from around the world. This wider reach increases the chances of securing funding compared to traditional methods.

2. Validation and Market Testing: Crowdfunding campaigns serve as a

validation tool for new product ideas, helping creators gauge market interest and demand. Successful campaigns demonstrate market viability and may attract further investment from traditional sources.

3. Community Engagement: Crowdfunding creates a sense of community and allows backers to participate in projects they are passionate about. Supporters often receive rewards or incentives in return for their contributions, fostering a sense of involvement and ownership.

4. Early Adopters and Brand Advocates: Crowdfunding campaigns can help generate early adopters and loyal brand advocates

who are invested in the project's success. These initial backers can provide valuable feedback and serve as ambassadors for the product or venture.

TIPS FOR SUCCESS:

To make the most of peer-to-peer lending and crowdfunding, consider the following tips:

1. Research Platforms: Explore different P2P lending platforms and crowdfunding websites to find the ones that align with your goals, risk tolerance, and investment preferences. Read reviews, evaluate their track records, and understand their fee structures and policies.

2. Diversify Investments: Spread your investments across multiple loans or crowdfunding projects to minimize risk and increase the potential for returns. This

strategy helps protect your capital and reduces the impact of any individual loan default or campaign failure.

3. Due Diligence: Conduct thorough research on borrowers or project creators before making investment decisions. Review their profiles, credit history, business plans, or project descriptions to assess their credibility and potential for success.

4. Stay Informed: Keep track of industry trends, regulatory changes, and updates from the P2P lending and crowdfunding sectors. Stay informed about any risks

associated with these platforms and adjust your investment strategy accordingly.

CONCLUSION:

Peer-to-peer lending and crowdfunding have transformed the way individuals and businesses access capital and generate funding. These online platforms offer new opportunities for investors to earn returns and for borrowers to secure financing outside the traditional banking system. By leveraging P2P lending and crowdfunding wisely, you can participate in the collaborative economy, support innovative projects, and potentially make money online. However, always remember to approach these platforms with a diligent and informed mindset, considering the risks and rewards associated with each opportunity.

FURTHER READING:

If you enjoyed this book, please consider reading one of the other books in the series:

Making Money Online: Book 1 (Understanding the Online Landscape)

Making Money Online: Book 2 (E-commerce and Online Retail)

Making Money Online: Book 3 (Freelancing and Remote Work)

Making Money Online: Book 4 (Content Creation and Monetization)

Making Money Online: Book 5 (Online Tutoring and Education)

Making Money Online: Book 6 (Online Surveys, Microtasks, and Rewards)

Making Money Online: Book 7 (Online Investments and Trading)

Making Money Online: Book 8 (Creating and Selling Digital Assets)

Making Money Online: Book 9 (Online Consulting and Coaching)

Making Money Online: Book 10 (Maximizing Online Income Opportunities)

All the books can be found on Amazon as Kindle and Paperback, or you can buy the complete edition which contains the full series in one book. The complete edition is available as Kindle, Paperback and exclusively as Hardback. You can find all the links in my book site: books.michaelmayaka.co.uk.

www.ingramcontent.com/pod-product-compliance
Lightning Source LLC
Chambersburg PA
CBHW040300220526
45473CB00002B/537